Birds

Julie Murray

Abdo
FAMILY PETS
Kids

abdopublishing.com

Published by Abdo Kids, a division of ABDO, PO Box 398166, Minneapolis, Minnesota 55439.
Copyright © 2016 by Abdo Consulting Group, Inc. International copyrights reserved in all countries.
No part of this book may be reproduced in any form without written permission from the publisher.

Printed in the United States of America, North Mankato, Minnesota.

052015

092015

 THIS BOOK CONTAINS
RECYCLED MATERIALS

Photo Credits: iStock, Shutterstock

Production Contributors: Teddy Borth, Jennie Forsberg, Grace Hansen

Design Contributors: Candice Keimig, Dorothy Toth

Library of Congress Control Number: 2014958552

Cataloging-in-Publication Data

Murray, Julie.

 Birds / Julie Murray.

   p. cm. -- (Family pets)

ISBN 978-1-62970-898-0

Includes index.

1. Birds--Juvenile literature. 2. Pets--Juvenile literature.   I. Title.

636.6'8--dc23

                   2014958552

Table of Contents

Birds

Birds make great family pets.

Many birds have **bright** colors.

Mia holds her parrot.

Some birds can say words.

Leo listens to his parakeet.

Some birds can't live alone.

Lovebirds live in **pairs**.

Birds need a large cage.

It has to be kept clean.

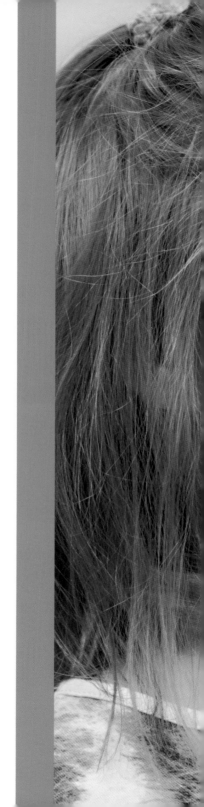

13

Birds need food.

They need water.

Birds need a place to sit.

Wooden sticks work well.

16

They need toys. They like bells, ladders, and swings.

Is a bird the right pet for your family?

Bird Supplies

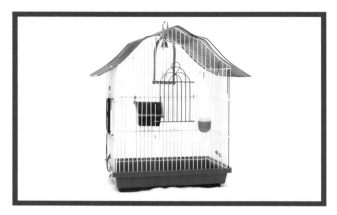

birdcage

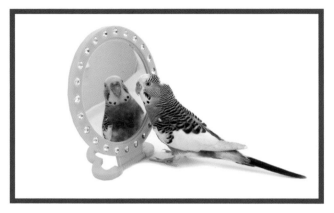

mirror

bird food

swing perch

Glossary

bright
having a very light and strong color.

pair
a set, or two of something.

Index

abdokids.com

Use this code to log on to abdokids.com and access crafts, games, videos, and more!

Abdo Kids Code:
FBK8980